THE COUNT YOUR CHANGE WIPE-OFF BOOK

D0963922

THE
COUNT YOUR
CHANGE
WIPE-OFF
BOOK

SCHOLASTIC INC.

New York Toronto London Auckland Sydney

HOW TO USE THIS BOOK

1. Study the QUICK COIN GUIDE pages to see how much each coin is worth.
2. Note how different coins put together can add up to the same amount.
3. Beginning with PENNY, fold the flap on the back cover over the answers and start adding your change.
4. Write the answers in the boxes **with a grease pencil or an erasable felt-tip pen.**
5. Check your answers. How did you do?
6. If your answers are correct, erase them with a damp cloth and go on to the NICKEL page, and so on.
7. If you missed some answers, go back and review the QUICK COIN GUIDE pages, then try the same page again.

GOOD LUCK!

ISBN 0-590-45694-6

Copyright © 1992 by FOUR HARTS, INC. All rights reserved. Published by Scholastic Inc.

20 19 18 17 16 15 14 13 12   89/9012/0

Printed in the U.S.A.
First Scholastic printing, August 1992

QUICK COIN GUIDE

1¢ =

5¢ = =

10¢ = =

10¢ = =

25¢ = =

QUICK COIN GUIDE

25¢ = =

50¢ = =

75¢ =

100¢
or
$1.00 =

P
E
N
N
Y

= 2¢

= 5¢

= 4¢

= 8¢

= 10¢

= 6¢

= 7¢

N
I
C
K
E
L

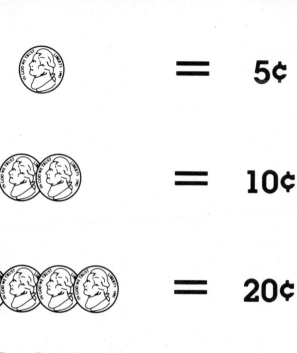

= 5¢

= 10¢

= 20¢

= 50¢

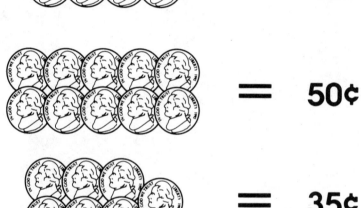

= 35¢

= 15¢

= 30¢

= 10¢

= 20¢

= 50¢

= 70¢

= 40¢

= 60¢

= 90¢

D
I
M
E

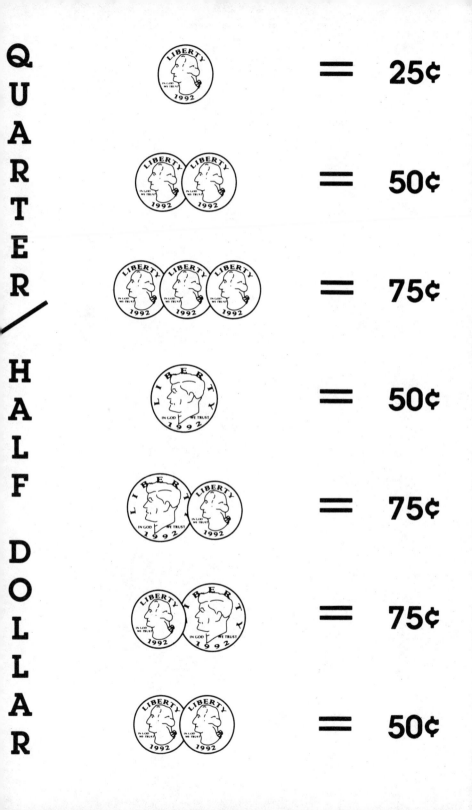

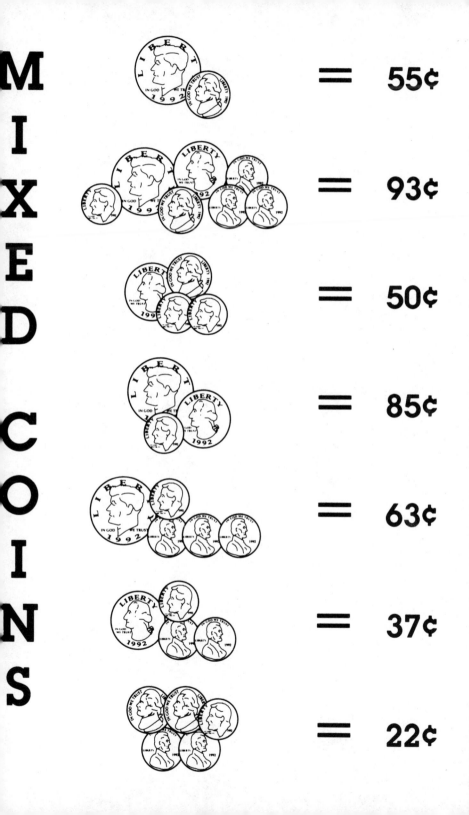

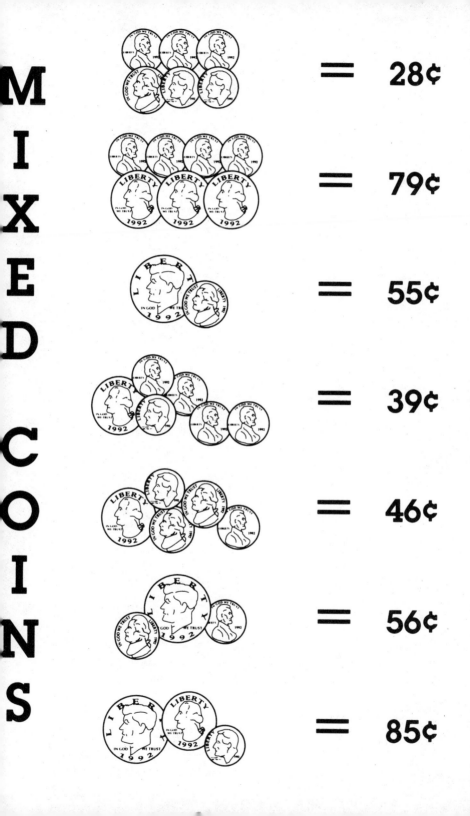

M

I

X

E

D

C

O

I

N

S

= 28¢

= 79¢

= 55¢

= 39¢

= 46¢

= 56¢

= 85¢